These Are the
Gifts I'd Like
to Give to You

———————— ■ ————————

This is a special collection
filled with wonderful wishes
and the most meaningful
kind of gifts that could
ever be given.

Within the words of this book,
I would like to give
these gifts to you.

Library of Congress Catalog Card Number: 99-16855
ISBN: 0-88396-524-0

Acknowledgments: Endless thanks are given to those who gave me an awareness of the value of the "gifts" contained in this book, and tremendous appreciation is felt for fellow writers whose wisdom fills these pages. This book is dedicated to three special gifts in my life: my wife, Carrie, and my sons, Jordan and Casey.

Poems and excerpts by Susan Polis Schutz appearing in this publication, Copyright © by Stephen Schutz and Susan Polis Schutz. All rights reserved.

Excerpt from "Little Gidding" in FOUR QUARTETS, Copyright © 1942 by T. S. Eliot and renewed 1970 by Esme Valerie Eliot, reprinted by permission of Harcourt, Inc.

A careful effort has been made to trace the ownership of writings used in this anthology in order to obtain permission to reprint copyrighted materials and to give proper credit to the copyright owners. If any error or omission has occurred, it is completely inadvertent, and we would like to make corrections in future editions provided that written notification is made to the publisher.

Library of Congress Cataloging-in-Publication Data

These are the gifts I'd like to give to you : a sourcebook of joy and
    encouragement / edited by Douglas Pagels.
        p.   cm.
    ISBN 0-88396-524-0 (alk. paper)
    1. Joy Quotations, maxims, etc. 2. Encouragement Quotations,
    maxims, etc. I. Pagels, Douglas.
    PN6084.J65T49 2000
    152.4'2--dc21   99-16855
                                                          CIP

Blue Mountain Press ®

SPS Studios, Inc.
P.O. Box 4549, Boulder, Colorado 80306

These Are the

GIFTS

I'd Like
to Give to You

A Sourcebook of
Joy and Encouragement

Edited by Douglas Pagels

Contents

The Gift of...

The Gift of Knowing that Beautiful Tomorrows Begin Today

Tomorrow is a beautiful road
that will take you right where
you want to go...

If you spend today walking away
from worry and moving toward
serenity; leaving behind conflict
and traveling toward solutions;
and parting with emptiness and
never giving up on your search
for fulfillment. If you can do
what works for you, your present
will be happier and your path will
be smoother. And best of all?

You'll be taking a step
into a beautiful future.

— Douglas Pagels

We shall not cease from exploration
And the end of all our exploring
Will be to arrive where we started
And know the place for the first time.

— T. S. Eliot

The Gift of
Good Advice

It is a funny thing about life.
If you refuse to accept anything
but the best, you very often get it.

— W. Somerset Maugham

Enjoy when you can,
and endure when you must.

— Goethe

I avoid looking forward or backward,
and try to keep looking upward.

— Charlotte Brontë

There are times when life isn't all
you want, but it's all you have. So
what I say is: Have it! Stick a
geranium in your hat and be happy!

— Anonymous

The Gift of Being Able to Deal with Your Difficulties

Have you got a problem?
Do what you can
where you are
with what you've got.

— Theodore Roosevelt

I am only one, but I am one.
I cannot do everything, but I can
do something. And what I can do,
that I ought to do.
And what I ought to do,
I shall do.

— Edward Everett Hale

I decided to do more
of what I wanted to do,
stopped doing many things
I didn't want to do, and
gave up worrying about those
things I had no control over.

— Anonymous

The Gift of Setting the Stage
for Good Things to Happen

All the world's a stage. And all men and women
merely players: They have their exits and entrances;
And one man in his time plays many parts.

— William Shakespeare

Find the thing meant for you
to do, and do the best you can.

— Henry Ward Beecher

Don't let life discourage you;
everyone who got where he is
had to begin
where he was.

— R. L. Evans

Go on deserving applause, and you
will be sure to meet with it.

— Thomas Jefferson

Make a triumph of every
aspect of your life.

— Susan Polis Schutz

The Gift of
Using Time Wisely

Nothing is worth more than this day.

— Goethe

When I think of how quickly time flies,
I am always sorry that I did not do better
yesterday or last year, because that
particular opportunity will never come
again. But I comfort myself with thinking
that the opportunity to do better next time
lies before me.

— Edward Chipman Guild

I know not what the future holds,
but I know who holds the future.

— Anonymous

Take care of the minutes, and the
hours will take care of themselves.

— Anonymous

The Gift of Hope

Out of the lowest depths there is
a path to the loftiest height.

— Thomas Carlyle

When you need some help to get through the
day; when you need a whole lot less to concern
you and a whole lot more to smile about...
sometimes you just have to remember:

It really is going to be okay. You're going to make
it through this day. Even if it's one step at a time.

Sometimes you just have to be patient and brave
and strong. If you don't know how, just make it
up as you go along. And hold on to your hope as
though it were a path to follow or a song to sing.

Because if you have hope,
   you have everything.

— Douglas Pagels

Hold on. Hope hard.

— Robert Browning

The Gift of Real Accomplishment

If we want to know what happiness is, we must seek it, not as if it were a pot of gold at the end of the rainbow, but among human beings who are living richly and fully the good life. If you observe a really happy man, you will find him building a boat, writing a symphony, educating his children, growing double dahlias in his garden. He will not be searching for happiness... he will have become aware that he is happy in the course of living twenty-four crowded hours in the day.

— W. Beran Wolfe

Remember that there is one thing better than making a living — making a life.

— Anonymous

Sometimes it's important to work for that pot of gold. But other times it's essential to take time off and to make sure that your most important decision in the day simply consists of choosing which color to slide down on the rainbow.

— Douglas Pagels

The Gift of Imagining the Possibilities

The principle business of life
is to enjoy it.

— Samuel Butler

Many of us have road maps we
envision for the course we think our
lives should take. It's important to get
headed in the right direction, but don't
get so caught up in the concerns over
your destination that you forget to
delight in the scenery of each new day.
Remember that some of the secret joys
of living are not found by rushing from
point A to point B, but by inventing
some imaginary letters along the way.

— Douglas Pagels

The truth is that everything
is a miracle and a wonder.

— Rabbi Barukh

Out of every earth day,
make a little bit of heaven.

— Ella Wheeler Wilcox

The Gift of Spreading Smiles Around

The sun, as we journey toward it,
casts the shadow of our burden behind us.

— Samuel Smiles

A smile is a curved line
that sets things straight.

— Anonymous

Life is a mirror.
If you frown at it,
it frowns back;
if you smile,
it returns the greeting.

— W. M. Thackeray

A smile is the light
in the window of your face
which tells people that
your heart is at home.

— Anonymous

The Gift of Being Enthusiastic!

You can do anything
    if you have enthusiasm.

— Henry Ford

I am unaware of anything
that has a right
to be called an impossibility.

— Thomas H. Huxley

We act as though comfort and luxury
    were the chief requirements of life, when
    all that we need to make us really happy
    is something to be enthusiastic about.

— Charles Kingsley

Nothing is so contagious as enthusiasm!
It is the genius of sincerity, and truth
accomplishes no victories without it.

— Anonymous

The Gift of Knowing that the Joy Is in the Journey

All life is an experiment. The more experiments you make, the better.

— Ralph Waldo Emerson

The truth is that it is natural,
as well as necessary, for every
man to be a vagabond occasionally.

— Samuel H. Hammond

This is a magnificent journey you're on.
Don't be afraid to explore unfamiliar
territory. If you do happen to get lost,
you will stumble across some of the
most interesting discoveries you will
ever make.

Wander down roads you've never explored
before and ones you'll never chance upon
again. Life isn't a travel guide to follow.
It's an adventure to undertake.

— Douglas Pagels

The Gift of Comprehending
What Others Are Going Through

Be kind. Everyone you meet
is fighting a hard battle.

— John Watson

One of the injustices of life is being judged by
others, when those judging might be guilty, as
well. Don't scrutinize people with a microscope;
view them from a comfortable distance. And allow
some room for compassion in the space that lies
between you.

— Douglas Pagels

Go beyond yourself and reach out to other
people with a sincere love, respect, caring,
and understanding of their needs.

— Susan Polis Schutz

Resolve to be: tender with the young,
compassionate with the aged,
sympathetic with the striving,
and tolerant of the weak and the wrong.
There will be times in your life
when you will have been all of these.

— Anonymous

The Gift of a Lifetime
of Learning

The best kind of learning curve
is an educated smile.

— Douglas Pagels

It isn't how little you know that matters,
but how anxious you are to learn.

— C. Newland

Learning is like rowing upstream:
not to advance is to drop back.

— Chinese Proverb

The one who graduates today
and stops learning tomorrow
is uneducated the day after.

— Anonymous

If we are wise, we never leave school.

— Horace Fletcher

The Gift of a Real Friend

A friend is one of the nicest things you can have, and one of the best things you can be. A friend is a living treasure, and if you have one, you have one of the most valuable gifts in life.

A friend is the one who will always be beside you, through all the laughter, and through each and every tear. A friend is the one thing you can always rely on; the someone you can always open up to; the one wonderful person who always believes in you in a way that no one else seems to.

A friend is a sanctuary.
A friend is a smile.

A friend is a hand that is always holding yours, no matter where you are, no matter how close or far apart you may be. A friend is someone who is always there and will always — always — care. A friend is a feeling of forever in the heart.

A friend is the one door that is always open. A friend is the one to whom you can give your key. A friend is one of the nicest things you can have, and one of the best things you can be.

— Douglas Pagels

The Gift of Helping
Those Around You

Ten rules for getting rid of the blues:
Go out and do something nice for
someone else, then repeat it nine times.

— Anonymous

Life is like a game of tennis: the
player who serves well seldom loses.

— Anonymous

He who, forgetting self, makes the object of
his life service, helpfulness and kindness to
others, finds his whole nature growing and
expanding, himself becoming large-hearted,
magnanimous, kind, sympathetic, joyous, and
happy; his life becoming rich and beautiful.

— Ralph Waldo Trine

Helping someone else
is the secret of happiness.

— Booker T. Washington

The Gift of Moving Beyond
Your Misfortunes

In the midst of misfortunes, it is well to remember that every mountain must have its valley, every oasis its desert, every rainbow its storm, and every day its night.

— Anonymous

If a door slams shut, it means
that God is pointing to an
open door further on down.

— Anna Delaney Peale

Misfortunes cannot always be avoided.
But they can be made easier — just by
knowing that they will be overcome.

— Seneca

The world is advancing.
Advance with it.

— Giuseppe Mazzini

The Gift of a Balance
Between Dollars and Sense

One of the hardest things about making
money last — is the ability to make it first.

— Anonymous

Money doesn't make you happy,
but it quiets the nerves.

— Sean O'Casey

More people should tell their dollars
where to go, rather than asking them
where they went.

— Anonymous

It's good to have money and the things
that money can buy, but it's good, too,
to check up once in a while and be sure
you haven't lost the things
money can't buy.

— George H. Lorimer

The Gift of Keeping Life's
Ups and Downs in Perspective

Every mountain means at least two valleys.

— Anonymous

I've had my trials and troubles.
The Lord has given me both vinegar
and honey, but He has given me
the vinegar with a teaspoon
and the honey with a ladle.

— Attributed to William Bray

If you want to live more, you must master the
art of appreciating the little, everyday blessings
of life. This is not altogether a golden world,
but there are countless gleams of gold to be
discovered in it.

— Henry Alford Porter

If you haven't all the things you want,
be grateful for the things you don't have
that you didn't want.

— Anonymous

The Gift of Welcoming
the Wonder

I walk the world in wonder.

— Oscar Wilde

Not knowing when the dawn will come,
I open every door.

— Emily Dickinson

And all the windows
of my heart
I open to the day.

— John Greenleaf Whittier

Each day brings with it the miracle of a new
beginning. Many of the moments ahead will
be marvelously disguised as ordinary days,
but each one of us has the chance to make
something extraordinary out of them.

— Douglas Pagels

Whatever has not happened in a thousand years
may happen in the next moment.

— Ladino

The Gift of Keeping
Worries Away

It is foolish to worry about
anything so temporary as today.

— Anonymous

Worry is like a rocking chair — it will
give you something to do, but it
won't get you anywhere.

— Anonymous

Nothing wastes more energy
than worrying. The longer one
carries a problem, the heavier
it gets. Don't take things too
seriously. Live a life of serenity,
not a life of regrets.

— Douglas Pagels

The words "peace" and "tranquility"
are worth a thousand pieces of gold.

— Chinese Proverb

The Gift of Being
the Best You Can Be

Sometimes you
think that you
need to be perfect
that you cannot
make mistakes
At these times
you put so much
pressure on yourself
I wish you
would realize
that you are
a human being —
like everyone else
capable of
reaching great potential
but not capable of
being perfect
So please
just do your best
and realize that
this is enough
Don't compare yourself
to anyone
Be happy to be
the wonderful
unique, very special
person that you are

— Susan Polis Schutz

The Gift of Paying
Attention to the Details

Most of us will never do great things,
but we can do small things in a great way.

— Anonymous

A great artist can paint a great picture
on a small canvas.

— Charles Dudley Warner

Admire your accomplishments.
Large or small, tremendous or
tiny, they contribute to the
well-being of this world. A little
light somewhere makes a brighter
light everywhere. A speck of
sand can turn into a pearl.

— Douglas Pagels

Buried deep in the maze of commonplace,
the pearl of true happiness lies. And he who
rejoices in little things, finds the pathway
that leads to the prize.

— Lucy M. Thompson

The Gift of Dressing
for Success

Of all the things you wear,
your expression is the most important.

— Anonymous

We must cut our coat according to our cloth,
and adapt ourselves to changing circumstances.

— Dean W. R. Inge

Self-respect is the noblest garment with which
a man may clothe himself, the most elevating
feeling with which the mind can be inspired.

— Samuel Smiles

When one has much to put in them,
a day has a hundred pockets.

— Friedrich Nietzsche

The Gift of Spiritual Handholds

Whatever is to make us better and happy,
God has placed either openly before us
or close to us.

— Seneca

Not all religion is to be found in the
church, any more than all knowledge
is found in the classroom.

— Anonymous

A coincidence may be God's way
of acting anonymously in your life.

— Anonymous

If your knees are knocking,
kneel on them.

— Anonymous

Life is fragile: Handle with prayer.

— Anonymous

The Gift of Asking, Believing, Receiving

I ask not for a lighter burden,
but for broader shoulders.

— Jewish Proverb

Do not pray for easier lives.
Pray to be stronger men. Do
not pray for tasks equal to
your powers. Pray for powers
equal to your tasks! Then the
doing of your work shall be
no miracle, but you shall be
the miracle.

— Phillips Brooks

I ask not for a larger garden,
but for finer seeds.

— Russell Herma Cornwell

Keep on sowing your seed, for you
never know which will grow —
perhaps it all will.

— Ecclesiastes 11:6

The Gift of Finding Out
How Much Fun It Can Be

Cheerfulness keeps up a kind of delight
in the mind, and fills it with a steady
and perpetual serenity.

— Joseph Addison

Angels fly because they
take themselves lightly.

— G. K. Chesterton

There aren't many things as therapeutic
as smiles and laughter. Whenever you
look at things in a lighter vein, it shows
that your heart is in the right place.

— Douglas Pagels

Every survival kit should include
a sense of humor.

— Anonymous

The Gift of Listening
to Your Heart

There are choices ahead which could change your life. Unfortunately, there aren't any crystal balls to provide the answers, telling you where to go or what to do. But it is true that centuries of wisdom have never improved on this advice:

Just listen to your heart.

— Douglas Pagels

We do not know where we are going, but we are on our way.

— Stephen Vincent Benét

Trust your intuition. Its sources spring from deep within the soul.

— Douglas Pagels

Every wakeful step, every mindful act is the direct path to awakening. Wherever you go, there you are.

— Buddha

The Gift of Understanding
What Makes You So Outstanding

People go abroad to wonder at the height
of mountains, at the huge waves of the sea,
at the long courses of the rivers, at the vast
compasses of the ocean... and they pass by
themselves without even imagining.

— Augustine of Hippo

What the world is for us
depends on what we are ourselves.

— Lewis G. Janes

Every individual is a marvel of
unknown and unrealized possibilities.

— W. G. Jordon

You're an original, an individual, a
masterpiece. Celebrate that; don't let
your uniqueness make you shy. Don't
be someone other than the wonder you
are. Every star is important to the sky.

— Douglas Pagels

What should I be but just what I am?

— Edna St. Vincent Millay

The Gift of Allowing
for More Kindness

How beautiful a day can be
when kindness touches it!

— Anonymous

Do not stop with doing necessary kindnesses;
the unnecessary ones are of greater importance.

— Anonymous

Shall we make a new rule of life
from tonight: Always try to be a
little kinder than is necessary?

— Sir James M. Barrie

In this world, you must be a bit too kind
in order to be kind enough.

— Pierre Carlet de Chamblain de Marivaux

The Gift of an Affinity for the Environment

Heaven is under our feet,
as well as over our heads.

— Henry David Thoreau

Do your part for the planet. Do all the things
you know you "should" do. Our grandchildren's
children will either have words of praise for our
efforts and our foresight, or words that condemn
us for forgetting that they must live here long after
we are gone. Don't overlook the obvious: This is
not a dress rehearsal. This is the real thing. Our
presence has an impact, but our precautions do,
too. And the environment means the world to us.

— Douglas Pagels

Stoop and touch the earth, and receive its
influence; touch the flower, and feel its life;
face the wind, and have its meaning; let the
sunlight fall on the open hand as if you could
hold it. Something may be grasped from them
all, invisible yet strong. It is the sense of a
wider existence — wider and higher.

— Richard Jefferies

The Gift of Recognizing Opportunity When It Knocks

To improve the golden moment of
opportunity and catch the good that
is within our reach is the great art of life.

— Samuel Johnson

Opportunity seems to have an uncanny
habit of favoring those who have paid
the price of years of preparation.

— Anonymous

Opportunities sometimes drop into
people's laps, but not until they get their
laps where opportunities are dropping.

— Mildred Seydell

There is an old saying that opportunity knocks
but once; yet history shows that this is not true.
Opportunities for happiness and progress may
come in different forms, but they are with us
daily. If those for which we seek seem not at hand
today, let us not despair. They will come again
and again, hopeful for the day we will be able
and ready to recognize and grasp them.

— Anonymous

The Gift of Courage

Courage is the greatest of all virtues,
because if you haven't courage,
you may not have an opportunity
to use any of the others.

— Samuel Johnson

We have a choice: to spend a lot of time
fighting for what we know is right, or
to just accept what we know is wrong.

We must stand up for our rights
and for the rights of others,
even if most people say we can't win.

— Susan Polis Schutz

Count your blessings,
not your troubles.
You'll make it through
whatever comes along.
Within you are so many
answers. Understand,
have courage, be strong.

— Douglas Pagels

The Gift of Knowing How
to Go with the Flow

Here is some gentle wisdom that will get you through just about anything: Appreciate, with all your heart, the best of life; do everything within your power to pass the tests of life; and learn how to live with the rest of life.

— Douglas Pagels

The deepest rivers
flow with the least noise.

— Curt

Cooperation is doing with a smile
what you have to do anyway.

— Anonymous

Things turn out best for the
people who make the best
of the way things turn out.

— Anonymous

The Gift of Being Optimistic

Very little is needed to make a
happy life. It is all within yourself,
in your way of thinking.

— Marcus Aurelius

Most of us can, as we choose,
make of this world either
a palace or a prison.

— Sir John Lubbock

Two men look out through
the same bars: One sees the
mud, and one the stars.

— Frederick Langbridge

The darkest hour is the best time to see
the stars. Keep your spirits up; you'll find
that optimism is very refreshing. The wisest
people on earth are those who have a hard
time recalling their worries... and an easy
time remembering their blessings.

— Douglas Pagels

The Gift of a Life Filled with Love

I am so glad that you are here —
it helps me to realize how
beautiful my world is.

— Goethe

Won't you come into the garden?
I would like my roses to see you.

— Richard Brinsley Sheridan

Love is the source of life.

— Susan Polis Schutz

Someone has written that love makes people
believe in immortality, because there seems
not to be room enough in life for
so great a tenderness.

— Robert Louis Stevenson

We are each of us angels with only
one wing. And we can only fly
by embracing each other.

— Luciano De Creschenzo

The Gift of Rising Up
to Meet Your Potential

If we can put a man on the moon,
you can see your way through
to where you want to be.
There is a way.
There is *always* a way.

— Douglas Pagels

Have the daring to accept yourself as a
bundle of possibilities, and undertake
the game of making the most of your best.

— Harry Emerson Fosdick

No one knows what he can do
until he tries.

— Publilius Syrus

If we did all the things we are
capable of doing, we would
literally astound ourselves.

— Thomas A. Edison

The Gift of Knowing What's Wrong and Doing What's Right

Do unto others as though you were the others.

— Anonymous

It is easier not to begin to go wrong
than it is to turn back
and do better after beginning.

— James A. Garfield

There is always a best way of doing everything.

— Ralph Waldo Emerson

The true realist is the person who sees
things both as they are, and as they can
be. In every situation there is the
possibility of improvement; in every life
the hidden capacity for something better.

— Lester B. Pearson

The Gift of Encouraging
a Child's Smile

Every... child on this earth has an overwhelming
desire to be loved, to be wanted, to be appreciated.
To the extent that we can fulfill this desire... will
we find happiness ourselves.

— Anonymous

Let the children be happy. Teach them to
fill their hearts with feelings of wonder and
to be full of courage and hope. Nothing
is more important than the sharing of this
moment in time. Hold their kite strings, make
their hearts sing, make their smiles shine.

Reflect their inner and outer beauty. Encourage
them to be in less of a hurry. Love them each
fleeting second. Try to have the patience of a
saint, and the understanding of one, too. Admire
them. Inspire them. And tell them in untold ways
what they mean to you.

— Douglas Pagels

Mankind is always happy for having
been happy; so that if you make them
happy now, you make them happy twenty
years hence by the memory of it.

— Sydney Smith

The Gift of Making
Each Day a Masterpiece

A life well lived is simply a compilation
of days well spent.

— Douglas Pagels

Time can't take away anything that has
already been given: Your treasures from
days gone by are treasures still; your
most precious memories will always be.

We learn, as we go along, that happiness
is not one big, beautiful jewel we can
hold — or lose — in our hands. Each one
of us is an hourglass. And in the course
of our lives, we get to keep the diamonds
that come our way among the passing sands.

— Douglas Pagels

Today is big
with blessings.

— Mary Baker Eddy

The Gift of Getting to Know Your Fellow Travelers

We must think of life as a journey... Let us think of ways in which we can make the journey more pleasant for others as well as for ourselves. Let us remember that life's journey is good, it is thrilling, and it can be made beautiful if we do our part.

— Seth Harmon

We desire to be classified according to our exceptional virtues; we are apt to classify others according to their exceptional faults.

— Henry Bates Diamond

Every man is entitled to be valued by his best moment.

— Ralph Waldo Emerson

I am going your way, so let us go hand in hand. You help me and I'll help you. We shall not be here very long... so let us help one another while we may.

— William Morris

The Gift of Being Patient
with the Problems of Life

You must try to get along
the best you can.

— Walt Whitman

When I want to consider a particular problem,
I open a certain drawer. When I have settled the
matter in my mind, I close that drawer and
open another. When I desire to sleep, I close
all the drawers.

— Napoleon

Have courage for the great sorrows of life and
patience for the small ones; and when you
have laboriously accomplished your daily task,
go to sleep in peace. God is awake.

— Victor Hugo

Make each new morning the opening door
to a better day than the one before.

— Anonymous

The Gift of Keeping Up the Good Work

Life without endeavor is like entering a
jewel mine and coming out with empty hands.

— Japanese Proverb

Lives of all great men remind us
We can make our lives sublime,
And, departing, leave behind us
Footprints on the sands of time.

— Henry Wadsworth Longfellow

He who would leave footprints in the sands
of time must be sure to wear work shoes.

— Anonymous

The reason a lot of people do not recognize
opportunity is because it usually goes around
wearing overalls, looking like hard work.

— Thomas A. Edison

I am a great believer in luck, and I find
the harder I work, the more I have of it.

— Stephen Leacock

The Gift of Living in
a More Forgiving World

As long as the world keeps spinning around,
none of its inhabitants will *ever* be able to raise
themselves up — by putting other people down.

— Douglas Pagels

Bigotry and intolerance are always the
inevitable earmarks of ignorance... while
the results of education are sympathy and
understanding. To talk about education
without compassion is like talking about
a crooked straight line.

— D. J. Sizoo

Wherever there is a human being, I see
God-given rights inherent in that being,
whatever may be the sex or complexion.

— William Lloyd Garrison

Every person, in whatever garb, or of whatever
station or origin, is deserving of a full need of
consideration and understanding. To determine
that everyone we meet receives from us a just
measure of civility, is a worthy ambition and
practice.

— Anonymous

The Gift of Honoring That
Person in the Mirror

To find yourself, think for yourself.

— Socrates

Until you mean something to yourself,
you can't be important to anyone else.
One must live the good alone-life in order
to grow and develop in one's own way.

— Grace Moore

Everyone sees you as you appear to be;
few realize what you really are.

— Niccolo Machiavelli

Don't ever be your own worst critic. Always try
to be your own best ally. There are times when
it helps to acknowledge that: "I am aware that
I am less than some people prefer me to be, but
most people are unaware that I am so much
more than what they see."

— Douglas Pagels

The Gift of Letting
Your Creativity Shine

Be creative!
You're the artist here.
You're the one who can
brush away the clouds
and make the sun shine.
Paint your own picture,
choose your own colors.
And forget all that
business about having to
stay between the lines.

— Douglas Pagels

Every artist dips his brush in his soul, and
paints his own nature into his pictures.

— Henry Ward Beecher

Expressing your creativity is done more by the
way you are living than by any other gesture.

— Douglas Pagels

To affect the quality of the day —
that is the highest of the arts.

— Henry David Thoreau

The Gift of Learning
from Mistakes

Experience is a good teacher,
but she sends in terrific bills.

— Minna Antrim

Life continually teaches. We eventually
catch on. Some of us have master's degrees
in subjects we never intended to take. And
through our experiences, we realize: It's
okay to make mistakes. It's okay to fall.
    It's a form of higher education.

— Douglas Pagels

Every man is a damn fool for at
least five minutes every day; wisdom
consists in not exceeding the limit.

— Elbert Hubbard

If you don't learn from your mistakes,
there's no sense making them.

— Anonymous

The Gift of
a Happy Home

He is happiest, be he king or peasant,
who finds peace in his home.

— Goethe

I had rather be on my farm
than be emperor of the world.

— George Washington

I had rather be shut up in a very modest cottage,
with my books, my family and a few old friends...
letting the world roll on as it likes, than to occupy
the most splendid post which any human power
can give.

— Thomas Jefferson

Make two homes for thyself...
One actual home... and another
spiritual home, which thou art
to carry with thee always.

— Saint Catherine of Siena

Home, in one form or another,
is the great object of life.

— Josiah Gilbert Holland

The Gift of a Long, Happy Life

It is magnificent to grow older —
if one keeps young while doing it.

— Henry Emerson Fosdick

Do not complain about old age.
It is a privilege denied to many.

— Anonymous

The more sand has escaped from the hourglass
of our lives, the clearer we should see through it.

— Jean Paul

Let every year make you a better person.

— Benjamin Franklin

May you live to be a hundred —
and decide the rest for yourself.

— Irish Blessing

The Gift of Knowing that Health Is True Wealth

Take care of yourself. Good health
is everyone's major source of wealth.

— Anonymous

If your pursuit of wealth causes you to
sacrifice any aspect of your health, your
priorities are turned around.

Your physical condition is your compass;
it will tell you if you are headed in the right
direction or if you're going astray. It's not
your checkbook, but *you* who is counted
on to be there for the people in your world.
Be farsighted. Weigh the differences. Think
of the prices to pay.

— Douglas Pagels

One way to live happily ever after
is not to be after too much.

— Anonymous

The Gift of Going Beyond the Ordinary and Achieving Extraordinary Results

Don't be afraid to go out on a limb.
That's where the fruit is.

— Anonymous

Behold the turtle; he makes progress
only when he sticks his neck out.

— James Bryant Conant

It is not because things are difficult
that we do not dare;
it is because we do not dare
that they are difficult.

— Seneca

If you do what you've always done,
you'll get what you've always gotten.

—Anonymous

The Gift of
Enjoying It All

There is no season such delight can bring
as summer, autumn, winter and the spring.

— William Browne

Talk with the year which is coming as with a friend
who is crossing your threshold to bring you gifts.
Say, I welcome you. Let me come close to you; let
me walk beside you and listen to all the secrets
which you keep in your great soul for my sharing....

If I breathe in your pure airs, if I live according to
those natural laws which govern you, if I accept the
spring, the summer, the autumn, and the winter of
life as perfect expressions...
then I, too, may grow....

— Ella Wheeler Wilcox

True wisdom is to be: always
seasonable, and to change
with a good grace in changing
circumstances.

— Robert Louis Stevenson

The Gift of a More
Peaceful World

Give me the money that has been spent in war and I will clothe every man, woman, and child in an attire of which kings and queens will be proud. I will build a schoolhouse in every valley over the whole earth. I will crown every hillside with a place of worship consecrated to peace.

— Charles Sumner

The more you're bothered by something that's wrong, the more you're empowered to change things and make them right. The more we follow that philosophy as individuals, the easier it will be to brighten our horizons outward from there, taking in our communities, our cultures, our countries, and the common ground we stand on.

The crucible of peace and good will is far too empty, and each of us must — in some way — help to fill it.

— Douglas Pagels

We must be the change
we wish to see in the world.

— Mohandas K. Gandhi

The Gift of
Lasting Happiness

Happiness is the feeling you're feeling
when you want to keep feeling it.

— Anonymous

The happy have whole days,
and those they choose.
The unhappy have but hours,
and those they lose.

— Colley Cibber

The world has enough sorrow of its own.
For us to add to it would be such a shame.
Sometimes it is difficult, but nothing is sweeter
than balancing out the bad that is beyond your
control with the goodness — and greatness —
that is within reach. Let us always try our best.

May we find our own special ways of making
happiness a permanent part of our lives,
rather than having it as an occasional guest.

— Douglas Pagels

You deserve a life of happiness.

— Susan Polis Schutz

The Gift of Lighting
Candles in the Lives of Others

If one life shines, the life next to it
will catch the light.

— Anonymous

Go out of your way to be good to an older person.
You'll discover that you can make somebody's entire
day with a smile, a phone call, some fresh-picked
daisies, or whatever it is you've got.

Our elders have so much to give to those who listen,
but they are the ones who deserve to receive. Don't
pass up the chance to brighten their lives. An old
adage reminds us that they need only a little, but
they need that little — a lot.

— Douglas Pagels

It was only a glad "good morning"
As she passed along the way,
But it spread the morning's glory
Over the livelong day.

— Anonymous

The Gift of Knowing
that Everything Will Be Okay

Have patience. Everything
is difficult before it is easy.

— Saadi

Nothing in life is to be feared.
It is only to be understood.

— Marie Curie

If the sun and moon should doubt,
They'd immediately go out.

— William Blake

He who has a why to live for
can bear almost any how.

— Friedrich Nietzsche

You have a future that is in the best of hands.
Plan accordingly.

— Douglas Pagels

The Gift of Gentle Words
in Difficult Times

The mantra to help you make it through:
"Need to, can do. Have to, will do."

— Douglas Pagels

If you can walk, you can dance.
If you can talk, you can sing.

— Zimbabwe Proverb

Although the world is full of suffering,
it is also full of the overcoming of it.

— Helen Keller

When life hands you a lemon,
squeeze it and start a lemonade stand.

— Anonymous

The Gift of Guilt-Free Relaxation

Rest is not idleness, and to lie on the grass under the trees on a summer's day, listening to the murmur of water, or watching the clouds float across the sky, is by no means a waste of time.

— John Lubbock

He does not seem to me to be a free man who does not sometimes do nothing.

— Cicero

Lying in bed would be an altogether perfect and supreme experience if only one had a colored pencil long enough to draw on the ceiling.

— G. K. Chesterton

The time you enjoy wasting is not wasted time.

— Bertrand Russell

The Gift of Climbing the Ladders
That Reach to Your Stars

Even if you can't just snap your fingers
and make a dream come true, you can
travel in the direction of your dream,
every single day, and you can shorten
the distance between the two of you.

— Douglas Pagels

It does not matter how slowly you go
as long as you do not stop.

— Confucius

As you keep growing and learning
striving and searching
it is very important
that you pursue your own interests
without anything holding you back
It will take time
to fully understand yourself
and to discover what you
want out of life
As you keep growing and learning
striving and searching
I know that the steps in your journey
will take you on the right path

— Susan Polis Schutz

The Gift of Believing
in Miracles

I swear to you there are divine things
more beautiful than words can tell.

—Walt Whitman

All change is a miracle to contemplate; but it
is a miracle which is taking place every instant.

— Henry David Thoreau

The invariable mark of
wisdom is to see the
miraculous in the common.

— Ralph Waldo Emerson

The sun, with all those planets
revolving around it and dependent
on it, can still ripen a bunch of
grapes as if it had nothing else
in the universe to do.

— Galileo Galilei

The Gift of Acquired Wisdom

If second thoughts came
before first thoughts, how
much wiser we would be.

— Anonymous

Life would be infinitely happier if we
could only be born at the age of 80
and gradually approach 18.

— Mark Twain

Life can only be understood backwards,
but it must be lived forwards.

— Sören Kierkegaard

What a fool does in the end,
a wise man does in the beginning.

— Spanish Proverb

The Gift of Getting Things Done

I arise in the morning torn between a desire
to improve the world and a desire to enjoy
the world. This makes it hard to plan the day.

— E. White

The great thing about life is that as long
as we live, we have the privilege of growing.

— Joshua Loth Liebman

The great thing in the world
is not so much where you are
but in what direction you are going.

— Oliver Wendell Holmes

Your life is a work in progress. That's
"progress" — as in always moving forward,
always reaching, always striving, always
making things better.

— Douglas Pagels

The Gift of Giving Yourself
Something Grand to Look Back On

The time will come when winter will
ask you what you were doing all summer.

— Henry Clay

Off in the distance, I see an old man sitting in a comfortable chair beside an open fireplace. No, this is not a picture of my father, or grandfather, facing life's sunset — it is myself.

I have decided now, in my days of prime, to be kind to that old man.... I am going to be kinder to the body he will have to use.... I am going to be more kind to the mind the old man will have to use. Like my body, I will try to keep it agile. It is said that old folks live in the past. I have resolved to give the old man some pleasant memories, some pleasant scenes to gaze upon. I want him to be able to look back and see deeds of kindness done, cheer brought into lonely hearts. I want him to look back upon some outstanding achievement.

I want to give the old man a quiet confidence
in the future.

— Anonymous

Old age is like anything else. To succeed
at it, you've got to start young.

— Anonymous

The Gift of Realizing Your Dreams

Follow your hopes and dreams while you can. While the
desire is burning. When the chance comes your way.
Don't be a ship that stays in the harbor, never straying
from its safety. Don't get tangled up with "maybe...
maybe someday." Too many folks will tell you that if
you spend your whole life waiting, "someday" arrives
too little, too late.

Maybe it's already a little later than it seems. If you
really want to do it, do it while you can.
    Be brave... and sail away on your dreams.

— Douglas Pagels

For the people who are always going to do things: The
road to Success lies along the path of Decision, and up
the hill of Endeavor, and across the bridge of Patience.
The road to Defeat lies through the valley of Pretty Soon
and the winding paths of Wait-a-While.

— Ella Wheeler Wilcox

The road to success is dotted with
many tempting parking places.

— Anonymous

There's no traffic jam on the extra mile.

— Anonymous

The Gift of Keeping Smiles Up
and Stress Levels Down

Life is really simple, but we insist
on making it complicated.

— Confucius

Learn how to say "No!" — and it will be of
more use to you than to be able to read Latin.

— C. H. Spurgeon

You don't have to be the one responsible for
making everything work. Believe me. The big
things are already taken care of: The sun will rise
in the morning, the stars will come out at night,
and — if you work it right — a child, someone you
love, or a dear, close friend, will share a special
smile with you — and make
everything wrong — right again.

— Douglas Pagels

There are only two things in the world to worry
over: The things you can control, and the things
you can't control. Fix the first, forget the second.

— Anonymous

The Gift of Making Today
Your Moment in Time

Don't make the mistake of letting
yesterday use up too much of today.

— Anonymous

Leave tomorrow
until tomorrow.

— German Proverb

Whether you're eighteen or eighty, I encourage
you to have the courage to find the magic in
this day. Go out of your way to appreciate the
deserving things here before you: people who
matter, places that will inevitably change, and
circumstances that get rearranged all too easily.

Do more than stop and smell the roses. Search them
out. Plant new seeds in the places you pass by. If
someone has made a difference in your life, let them
know. And remember that there's more to appreciate
in this moment than we realize. Believe me:

Years from now, the truth of this will shine. And
one of your sincere regrets will be not knowing
how good you had it... at the time.

— Douglas Pagels

The Gift of an Angel by Your Side

May you always have an angel by your side •
Watching out for you in all the things you do •
Reminding you to keep believing in brighter
days • Finding ways for your wishes and dreams
to come true • Giving you hope that is as
certain as the sun • Giving you the strength of
serenity as your guide • May you always have
love and comfort and courage •

And may you always have an angel by your
side • Someone there to catch you if you fall •
Encouraging your dreams • Inspiring your
happiness • Holding your hand and helping
you through it all • In all of our days, our lives
are always changing • Tears come along as
well as smiles • Along the roads you travel,
may the miles be a thousand times more lovely
than lonely • May they give you gifts that never,
ever end: someone wonderful to love and a
dear friend in whom you can confide • May
you have rainbows after every storm • May you
have hopes to keep you safe and warm •

And may you always have an angel
by your side •

— Douglas Pagels

The Gift of Keeping
Young at Heart

Genius is childhood recaptured.

— Charles Baudelaire

It is familiarity with life that makes time
speed quickly. When every day is a step
into the unknown, as it is for children,
the days are long with the gathering
of experience.

— George Gissing

I am not young enough
to know everything.

— Sir James M. Barrie

I think it would help if every now and then
I let the child that shines within me
live in harmony with the adult
I'm required to be.

— Douglas Pagels

The Gift of Faith Having a Place in Your Life

As a knot appears unexpectedly in a thread, so disappointment blocks the smoothness of life. If a few deft strokes can untangle the skein, life continues evenly. But if it cannot be corrected, then it must be quietly woven into the design. Thus, the finished piece can still be beautiful — even though not as perfect as planned.

— Anonymous

We sleep, but the loom of life never stops and the pattern which was weaving when the sun went down — is weaving when it comes up tomorrow.

— Henry Ward Beecher

The sunrise never failed us yet.

— Celia Thaxter

For any weaving that needs to be done, God sends the threads.

— Italian Proverb

The Gift of 24 Beautiful Hours

Everything is only for a day.

— Marcus Aurelius

How mankind defers from day to day the
best it can do, and the most beautiful things
it can enjoy, without thinking that every day
may be the last one, and that lost time is
lost eternity.

— Max Müller

You can do more with five minutes now
than with a thousand years after you are dead.

— Anonymous

Make each day useful and cheerful
and prove that you know the worth
of time by employing it well.

— Louisa May Alcott

If God adds another
day to our lives, let
us receive it gladly.

— Seneca

The Gift of Using Pride
as a Guiding Light

It is the greatest of advantages
to enjoy no advantage at all.

— Henry David Thoreau

To really know what success means,
earn it. Don't rely on some elevator
to take you there. The easiest lessons
to remember are the ones you learn
the hard way. The higher the floor
you want to reach, the more important
it is to take the stairs.

— Douglas Pagels

Worthy things happen
to the worthy.

— Plautus

Do the thing that is right
even when the boss isn't looking,
because the boss isn't a criterion.

The real boss is standing alongside you
every moment of your life.

— Alfred P. Haake

The Gift of Controlling
Your Own Destiny

If you think you can, or think
you can't, you're probably right.

— Mark Twain

Clear your mind of can't.

— Samuel Johnson

The difference between perseverance
and obstinacy is that one is motivated
by a strong will, and the other by a
strong won't.

— Anonymous

We can always do more and be more than we
think we can. Let's *think* less and *imagine* more.

— Douglas Pagels

The Gift of Living in a Way That Is Rewarding to You

The life of every man is a diary in which he means to write one story, and writes another; and his humblest hour is when he compares the volume as it is with what he vowed to make it.

— Sir James M. Barrie

Every job is a self-portrait of the person who did it. Autograph your work with excellence!

— Anonymous

In the story of your life, write the best book you can. Have pages on understanding and tales of overcoming hardships. Fill your story with romance, adventure, poetry, and laughter. Make each chapter reflect time well spent. Meet your obligations, but take time to greet your aspirations. If you live up to your potential, you'll never have to live down any disappointment.

— Douglas Pagels

The Gift of Hanging In There
and Holding On

The difficult we do immediately.
The impossible takes a little longer.

— Charles Alexandre de Calonne

When you must,
you can.

— Jewish Proverb

You don't have to know *how* to sing.
It's feeling as though you *want* to
that makes the day worthwhile.

— Coleman Cox

Those who wish to sing
always find a song.

— Swedish Proverb

The Gift of Appreciating
Life to the Fullest

I may be uncertain about exactly where
I'm headed, but I am very clear regarding
this: I'm glad I've got a ticket to go on this
magnificent journey.

— Douglas Pagels

There is no cure for birth and death
save to enjoy the interval.

— George Santayana

That it will never come again
Is what makes life so sweet.

— Emily Dickinson

It is a grand thing to live — to open the eyes
in the morning and look out upon the world;
to drink in the pure air and enjoy the sweet
sunshine; to feel the pulse bound and the being
thrill with the consciousness of strength and
power in every nerve. It is a good thing simply
to be alive, and it is a good world to live in,
in spite of the abuse we are fond of giving it.

— Anonymous

The Gift of Some of the Most Wonderful Wisdom of All

It is never
too late
to be
what you
might have been.

— George Eliot

We can bring so many blessings
into our lives just by realizing
that it is *never too late*. Before
you turn the page on this day,
make a pact with yourself to
untie the ribbons and open the
gifts we are given in this life. Do
ordinary things in extraordinary
ways. Have health and hope and
happiness! Live a full life on this
earth, understand your real worth,
and wish on all your stars.

And don't ever forget, for even a day,
how very special
you are.

— Douglas Pagels

The Gift of Many
Happy Returns

The world is round, and the place
which may seem like the end
may also be only the beginning.

— Ivy Baker Priest

The game of life is a game of
boomerangs. Our thoughts, deeds,
and words return to us sooner or
later with astounding accuracy.

— Anonymous

Then give to the world
the best you know
And the best will come
back to you.

— Henry Wadsworth Longfellow

Author-Editor Profile

Douglas Pagels has been one of SPS Studios' favorite writers for many years. His philosophical sayings and sentiments on friendship and love have been translated into seven languages and shared with millions of people worldwide in notecards, calendars, and his previous books. He lives in the mountains of Colorado with his wife and two sons.